Easy Sock Puppets!

Tips & Techniques for Fabulous Fun

Puppets created by
Raffaella Dowling

Photography by F. William Lagaret

Text by Jessica Dowling

Mud Puddle Books
NEW YORK

Easy Sock Puppets:
Tips & Techniques for Fabulous Fun

Puppets Created by Raffaella Dowling
Photography by F. William Lagaret
Text by Jessica Dowling

Copyright © 2009 by Mud Puddle Books, Inc.

Published by
Mud Puddle Books, Inc.
54 W. 21st Street
Suite 601
New York, NY 10010
info@mudpuddlebooks.com

ISBN: 978-1-60311-203-1

Printed in China

ontents

Gallery

Introduction

For many years, children have been making their own toys. Using bits of paper, scraps of fabric, and other found objects, wonderful playthings can be made right in your own home. The advantage over store-bought toys is that these homemade trinkets have a special personality that you create. Sock puppets are a fantastic do-it-yourself toy. They are simple enough for children to create, yet adults can get in on the fun too! Sock puppets can be as simple or elaborate as you'd like. The creation of these charming little creatures is a wonderful family project for everyone to enjoy. Let's get started!

Getting Started

To get started, you'll need a sock. Used socks are fine to use (washed, of course!), but you may want to start off with brand new socks. If the used socks are too worn, your poor puppet will fall apart! Choose a color sock that will complement the design of your puppet. Solid color socks usually work best. Consider a green sock for a dragon sock puppet, or a brown sock for a dog puppet. Experiment with patterned socks, too! For instance, a red sock with black polka dots would make a great ladybug puppet!

It is easiest to design your puppet with the sock on your hand, so that you can see the shape of it and visualize it's design. Start off by putting the sock on your hand so that the tips of your fingers are where the toes should go, and the heel is at the top of your wrist. Your thumb acts as the puppet's jaw, allowing you to make it "talk". Carefully, with a pencil, you can mark on the puppet where you'd

Make Your Own Finger Puppets! 5

like your design elements to go. Take the sock off your hand before you actually start work on the puppet. As fabric is permeable (meaning liquids will pass through it), the glue, paint, and ink you use could bleed through the sock and get all over your hand, or you could prick yourself while sewing things on to your puppet. After you add your embellishments, allow the sock puppet to dry thoroughly before using it. If you use glue or paint on your puppet, you will want to prevent it from sticking to itself while drying. So, carefully slip the sock over an empty soda bottle. This will allow the sock to keep its form while it dries.

Once you have embellished the sock to your liking, you officially have a sock puppet! Use sock puppets to create elaborate puppet shows for your family, to play make-believe with your friends, or give them as special homemade gifts for any occasion. These handmade treasures offer so much fun in their creation and use!

Materials:

Socks Choose a size sock that will comfortably fit your hand.

Scissors Plain scissors or pinking shears for creating fun edges. Keep in mind that using scissors to cut things like felt will dull the blades over time, so keep a pair of scissors just for puppet crafting!

Colored Felt Use this stiff fabric to cut out shapes that you can attach to your puppets. Great for cutting out ears for dog or cat puppets, or wings for flying friends like dragons or bugs. When gluing felt, a little bit of glue will do the trick. Oversaturating it will make it heavy and hard to stick.

Craft foam These easy-to-work-with sheets of colored foam can be cut out and used for nearly anything on a sock puppet.

Buttons Use as eyes, noses, or mouths, or just as buttons on the puppet's clothing.

Make Your Own Finger Puppets!

Needle and Thread (Always ask an adult for help when using these) Use to attach pieces to your puppets, or to stitch designs. Be careful not to sew the sock shut!

Pom-Poms Can be used as noses, eyes, or even fur! You can make a clever sheep puppet using white pom-poms as wool.

Baby Socks Tiny socks such as ones made for dolls or babies can be a cute and creative addition to your materials. Use them as the ears on puppets or as mittens!

Fabric Paint/Markers Can be used to draw directly on your puppet. Markers won't work well on dark colored socks, so, in that case, opt for fabric paint ("puffy paint").

Pipe Cleaners Bend these to make hair or whiskers. They can also be bent into mustaches, flowers, or anything else you can think of! Try using them as antennae on bee or bug puppets, or as arms on a snowman puppet.

Googly Eyes Obviously, these can be used as eyes, but don't stop there! How about using them as the spots on a leopard puppet?

Cardboard or **Craft paper** This can be cut and used much like felt, but with less permanent results. Try cutting out cardboard to make arms and legs for your puppet.

Sequins Sequins can be used in a lot of ways: as the spots on an animal, as eyes, or to create interesting textures and designs.

Ribbon Thin ribbons may be used as funky hair or fur, while wider ribbons can be wrapped around your sock to create different clothing.

Fabric Scraps Fun and colorful scraps of fabric can be used to craft a variety of items and effects for your sock puppets. Try cutting a scrap of fabric to make a fun necktie for your puppet. Use your creativity!

Yarn Yarn is a great material for adding texture to your puppet. A bunch of yarn tied together makes an excellent mane or tail on a horse puppet.

 **Craft Glue** Use this to attach most of your design elements to the sock puppet. Some heavier items may also need a stitch or two from your needle and thread to stay attached. Be patient, and see what works.

Glitter To add sparkle and flair to your creations.

Popsicle Sticks As arms and legs, or try making a "fan" of orange, red and brown painted popsicle sticks for an impressive tail on a turkey puppet!

Feathers Useful for creating bird puppets, or for interesting fashion statements!

Beads Can be used as eyes, or buttons on clothing. Can also be used to add elaborate beaded patterns on your puppets.

Many of these items are optional, and feel free to add your own items to this list. The real fun in making sock puppets is using your imagination!

GALLERY
OF
FUN IDEAS

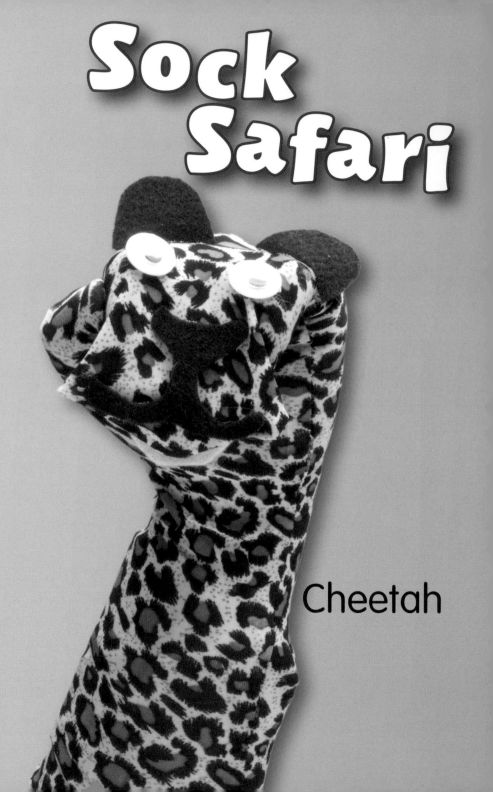

Sock Safari

Cheetah

Python

Lion

Zebra

Monkey

CREEPY

Bee

CRAWLERS

Ladybug

Spider
and Prey

Butterfly

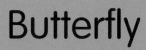

Garden Puppets

Sunflower

Daisy

Weed

Puppet Pets

Poodle

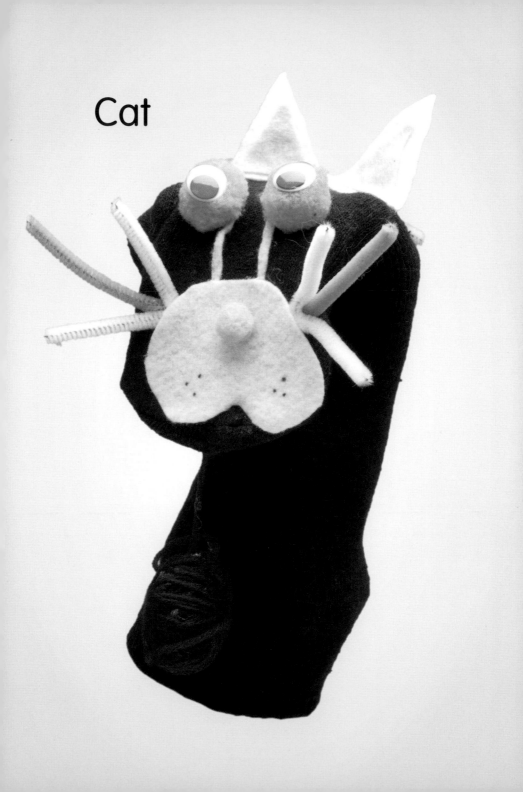

Cat

Dog

Easter Bunny

Snowman

Barnyard

Buddies

Cow

Horse

Pig

Chick

Snack Puppets

Drink

Burger

Pizza

Fantasy

Socks

Princess

Dragon

Unicorn

SPORTY

Football

SOCKS

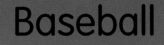

Baseball

Basketball

Tennis

Under the

School of Fish

Sea Socks

Shark

Turtle

Mermaid

Octopus